HAMPSHIRE DIALECT

A selection of words and anecdotes
from around Hampshire

by
Linda Fernley

BRADWELL
BOOKS

Published by Bradwell Books
9 Orgreave Close Sheffield S13 9NP
Email: books@bradwellbooks.co.uk

British Library Cataloguing in Publication Data:
a catalogue record for this book is available from the British Library.

1st Edition

ISBN: 9781909914322

Print: Gomer Press, Llandysul, Ceredigion SA44 4JL

Design and artwork by: Andrew Caffrey

Photograph Credits: ©Linda Fernley and where indicated Hampshire Arts and Museum Service.

My thanks go to Hampshire Arts and Museum Service for permission to use many of the photographs produced in this book, and to Winchester and Farnborough Libraries for their help and advice.

'I do always look towards Hampshire and plan my return. I'm sure it'll happen one day'.

COLIN FIRTH

As Mr Darcy in Jane Austen's *Pride and Prejudice*, Colin Firth stole the hearts of many viewers!

Jane Austen herself was a native of Hampshire.

Introduction

Hampshire, the largest county in south-east England and the third largest UK 'shire', is the birthplace of all three of the British Forces: the Army still resides in Aldershot; the RAF began life in Farnborough, my home town and one which still plays an important part in UK aviation; and the coastal towns of Portsmouth and Southampton have strong links with the Royal Navy. Hampshire's county town, Winchester, was historically the capital of England, and is still home to the largest medieval cathedral in Europe.

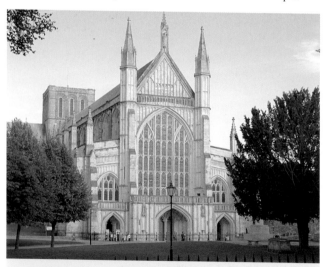

Winchester – the largest medieval cathedral in Europe

Despite a large number of populated towns and cities, a huge 45 per cent of Hampshire is taken up with two National Parks – the South Downs and the unique New Forest – and there's no shortage of very charming villages and hamlets.

Although a Midlander myself, I've lived in or around Hampshire for several decades, and am still discovering fascinating aspects about its places, people and dialect. Hampshire is often left out of dialect discussions; there's a general belief that it's a 'posh' county, whose inhabitants speak in a 'Queen's English' accent. However, in my experience use of 'Estuary English' – a halfway-house between cockney and standard English – is more common and, also contrary to popular belief, very few people in Hampshire use a west country 'oo arr' accent or dialect!

In the early 19th century, people living in rural south-west Hampshire, particularly the New Forest, spoke a dialect which is now rarely heard. You can still find traces of words peculiar to the area, and the accent itself has changed little but nowadays you're not likely to hear someone ask, *'Wair did ur cum vrom?'* ('Where did she come from?') or *'Bist dhee gwein too?'* ('Are you going, too?'), or *'Haih, loo see, dhaier's a scuggee muggins zittin on t' gaalay-baagur!'* (Look, see, there's a squirrel sitting on the scarecrow')!

Sadly, along with many other local dialects around the British Isles, the use of a Hampshire dialect has steadily decreased as the population has became more mobile over the past 75 years. So the following glossary is a selection of words taken from what older local Hampshire people either remember or still use, and from a collection of New Forester's dialect recorded mainly at the turn of the last century.

After the glossary, you'll find snippets about Hampshire life that I hope give a flavour of the rich diversity of the county, both past and present.

Linda Fernley 2014

The Hampshire Flag

Glossary

A

Aaeel – ale

Aaf – off

Aan't – haven't

Aarchurd – orchard

Aardinury – ordinary

Aardur – order

Aarkurd – awkward

Addur – after

Adhurt – across

Ad'n – had not

Aess – to ask, asked

Affeared – afraid

Afoar – before

Agg – egg

Aij – edge

Aist – east

Ait – eat

Aul – all

Av – have

Avert – across

Avoarhaand – before the event

Avroze – frozen, icy (of weather or conditions)

Awaaee – away

By 1790 Hampshire Hog (or 'ampshire 'og) was used in jest to describe a Hampshire person, the county being famous for 'a fine breed of hogs, and the excellency of the bacon made there'!
Creative Commons

B

Baakay – tobacco

Baarur – barrow

Baavin – bundle of small boughs

Bagg – beg

Baggur – beggar

Baich – beech

Baid – bad

Baif – beef

Bailey – more properly a bailiff, one who acted as an agent or steward of a landlord

Bain – bean

Baint – aren't, isn't

Bair – beer

Baird – beard

Baist – beast

Bar – a pound (currency)

Barn – born

Baug – bog

Bebee, bibee – baby

Bee – am, are, be

Bellur – bellow

Beskit – basket

Bin – been

Blaakay – blackbird

Blaid – shaft of a cart

Blakdhaarn – sloe bush
(sloes are used to make a type of gin)

Blather – a fuss, uproar

Blood-turnip – beetroot

Bob – shilling

Bobbeen – robin

Bond – band

Booay – boy

Boouth – both

Bottom – hollow, low-lying land

Bout – about

Brichin – a strap around horse's quarters

Bridewell – gaol, after Bridewell Palace in London, a residence of Henry VIII that later became a poor house/prison

Brimstone – a type of moth

But – boot

Butturvloi – butterfly

C

Caark – cork

Caarn – corn, wheat

Caarner – corner

Caas'n or caint – can't

Caat – caught

Cackleberry – egg

Caddle – muddle

Chaik – cheek

Chaisnut – chestnut

Chandler – a dealer in soap and candles

Chawbacon – an unsophisticated person; a bumpkin or yokel

Chiffay – chaffinch

Childaag – chilblain

Chillern – children

Chimblay, chimlay – chimney

Chinkay – chaffinch

Chiselbob – woodlouse

Chock – block of wood

Cruncheon – informal evening meal

Churching – a blessing ceremony for a new mother, before which it was considered improper for her to go out or receive visitors!

Claak -clock

Clain – clean

Clot – turf

Clum – handle clumsily

Cockleert – cock-crow, daybreak

Collect, the – a short general prayer

Coors – of course

Coos'n, or coosint – could not

Cooud – cold

Coout – coat

Cordner – more properly cordwainer; a shoemaker

Corral – to hang a kettle on

Craitur – creature

Cud – could

Cuttay – wren

Friendly Society Parade, East Street, Havant
Hampshire Arts and Museum Service

D

Daag – dog

Daartur – daughter

Daid – dead

Deich – ditch

Dhaier – there

Dhaiuf – thief

Dhaut – thought

Dhay – they, those, these

Dheen – thin

Dheezelf – yourself

Dhem – them, those

Dhenk – think

Dhetzh – thatch

Dhik – thick

Dhin – then

Dhing – thing

Dhink – think

Dhum – thumb

Dhurzelvz – themselves

Diddee/diddeecay – gypsy

Dimmet, dimpsey – dusk

Dipchick – a moorhen

Dirn – doorframe

Dishwasher – wagtail

Doaant, doaan – don't

Draap – drop

Draash – thrash, thresh

Drang – a narrow lane or alleyway between buildings

Dreckly – directly, straight away

Drei – dry

Driin – drain

Droa – throw

Droo – through

Dunnoa – don't know

Dus'n – doesn't

J Nesbit, Gosport Market Gardener, with horse and cart, c.1910
Hampshire Arts and Museum Service

E

Ee – he
Eef – if
Eer – hear
Eerd – heard
Ees – yes
Eet – yet
Ei – I
Eier – higher
Eirun – iron
Em – them
Emmet – ant
En – him
Enny wen – at any time
Er – ever
Erm – arm
Ess – ass
Extray – extra

F

Faarist – forest
Faivur – fever
Feesh – fish
Fell – fail

Feller – fellow, chap

Figgety pudden – plum-pudding, the forerunner of Christmas Pudding

Foar – before

Foaray – pinafore

Foar-haars – leading horse in a team

Fust – first

Fuzz buzz – traveller's joy

Wrens loading torpedoes onto the HMS Dolphin, Gosport
Hampshire Arts and Museum Service

G

Gaaeet – gate

Gaalay-baagur (or gallibagger) – scarecrow

Gaffer (and granfer) – grandfather

Gakeing – daydreaming

Gaun – dress

Gawermush – policeman

Gee, gi – give

Gel – girl

Gerdin – garden

Gev – given

Gi – give

Girt – great, big, large

Glaid – glad

Goosegogs – gooseberries

Gowk – cuckoo

Grammer – grandmother

Gress – grass

Groun – the fields

Grunt – grumble

Gurt – great, as in big

Gwein – part, going

H

Haaee – hat

Haalur – hollow

Haarn – horn

Haars, has – horse, pony

Haast – has

Haih! – eh! What!

Happen – maybe

Hazel poles – slender branches that grow upwards from the base of a coppiced hazel tree

Hef – half

Heidee-hoop – hide-and-seek

Heidin – hiding, thrashing

Heil – bundle of wheat

Herd – hard

Hervist – harvest

Het – heat

Het – hit

Heth – heath

Hid – head

Hij – hedge

Himp – hemp

Hin – hen

Hizzelf – himself

Hob – potato-pit

Hooum – home

Hoss, has – horse

Hous – house

Houzinz – houses

Decorated wagon, horse and group of people from the RAOB
(a charitable organisation) Winchester, 1922.
Hampshire Arts and Museum Service

I

Id – head

Idhout – outside

Id'n – isn't

I'll count – I suppose, I concede

I'll own – I admit, I acknowledge, I'll own up to

In – him

Insek – insect

Irrjin – engine

J

Jillay staak – gilliflower (type of carnation)

Jist – just

Joaay – a threepenny-bit

Job – difficulty

Joppety-joppety – in a state of nervous anxiety, jittery

K

Kees – kiss

Kent – can't

Kep – kept

Kich – catch

Kiddil – kettle

Kist – an ancient burial mound

Kiwur – cover

Kushti – good

L

Laang – long

Laeun – lane

Laif – leaf

Laig – leg

Laiv – leave

Leat – a stream

Leeray – empty (usually referring to hunger)

Leik – such as

Lid – lead

Limber – slim or slender (of a person)

Long – along

Loo see – look you

Low – allow, think, dare say

Lug – pole or perch

Sailmakers in the loft of Ratsey and Lapthorn, Gosport, 1934.
Shipbuilding and its associated trades used to be a very important
part of Hampshire life.
Hampshire Arts and Museum Service

M

Maaeed – girl

Maarnin – morning

Maistur – master

Mait – meat

Mallyshag – caterpillar

Mast – beech-nuts and acorns

Mauz – heap of corn in the straw

Mazed – crazy, mad, mentally unbalanced

Meddur – meadow

Mei – my

Meil – mile

Meind – remember

Mezelf – myself

Mid – might

Mid be – maybe

Mid'n – might not

Mimray – memory

Moak – donkey

Moast – very

Mommet – a scarecrow

Moour – more

Mooust – most

Mooustly – generally

Mum – ma'am

Mump – stroll, wander
Muss – must
Muss'n – must not

N

Naarth – north
Naist – nest
Nammet – lunch, usually taken by a labourer to eat at his place of work
Naut – nothing
Nestay – nasty
Niwur – never
Noad – knew, known
Nog – chunk of wood
Noo – no
Nudhin – nothing
Numshon – luncheon
Nus – nurse

O

Oa – of
Oam – home
Oap – hope
Offin – often

Oi – I, and yes
Ollay – holly
Ondoo – undo
Ood – wood
Ool – wool
Oolln – woollen
Oomun – woman
Oss – horse
Oun – hound
Ourn – ours
Ous – house

The preparations for D-Day, Gosport
Hampshire Arts and Museum Service

P

Paakit – pocket

Pag – peg

Paipul – people

Pait – peat

Palmer – caterpillar

Pay – pea

Pecty – covered with little spots of decay

Pinchfart – mean, tight

Pinnee – pinafore

Plaaee – play

Plaes – place

Plag – plague

Plaiz – please

Poodin – pudding

Pook – heap of hay

Pus – purse

Pyooit – lapwing

Q

Quag – bog or marshy area

Qwair – queer

Qweiut – quiet

Qwid – cud

R

Raabit – rabbit

Raaeel – rail

Raaeen – rain

Rail – real

Raip – reap

Randy – rustic celebration, often for a wedding or harvest

Rayed – dressed

Reit – right, thoroughly, quite

Rick – stack

Routle – to rummage (like a pig in straw)

Ruchtee – saddle-chain for a cart

Ruff – roof

Thanksgiving Service, St Vincent's Barracks, Gosport, 8 May 1945.
Hampshire Arts and Museum Service

S

Saart – sort

Saium – same

Scraich – screech

Scuggee muggings – squirrel

Seed – seen

Shaart – short

Shaat – shall

Shaat'n – shall not

Shrammed – frozen or cold to the bone

Shuffler – man employed in a farmyard

Sillir – cellar

Slug-abed – sluggard, lazy person

Smellfox – anemone

Smert – smart

Snag – sloe

Snoa – do you know

Snoch – notch

Sowbugs – woodlice

Spaik – speak

Speiur – spire

Spek – expect

Spoaz – suppose

Spreathed – red raw, rough – usually of hands

Squeiur – squire

Staarlin – starling

Staarm – storm

Stabble – to walk about aimlessly

Sterlyng – starling

Stook – stack of twelve sheaves of wheat or similar in a field

Stooun – stone

Straaeh – stretch

Stray – straw

Strickle – block upon which a blade, usually a scythe or sickle, was sharpened

Stroy – destroy, kill off

Sucker – young colt

Summat – something

Swaid – swede

Swait – sweet

T

T' – the

Taablish – fairly well

Taaeek – take

Taaeel – tail

Taak – talk

Taarbul – terribly

Taarmint – torment

Taebul – table

Taffety – fanciful

Taichur – teacher

Taieh – teach

Taitay – potato

Tallow – animal fat used to make soap and candles

Tedn't – it isn't

Teit – tight

Tell – count

Tetchy – irritable

Tiddee – potato

'Tiddin, 'tiddn't – isn't

Tithe – tax levied on crops and cattle, specifically one-tenth

Tiz – it is

Toad – told

T'odher – the other

Too – till

Toordz – towards

Tooud – toad, and told

Traaeen – train

Trash – thrush

Tremenjus – tremendous

Trivet – tripod of iron for holding cooking vessels over the fire

Tugz – metal piece on horse collars

Turmit (and turxnit) – turnip or occasionally swede

Tut-work – piece-work, paid for by the number of units produced

Twoald – tell, told

U

Un – him
Unrayed – undressed
Ur – her, them, or

Timber cutters in Bramshill Park photographed with their saws
and traction engine, late 19th century. Bramshill is now home
to the UK's largest Police Staff College.

Hampshire Arts and Museum Service

V

Vaalur – value
Vaardin – farthing
Vaarist – forest
Vaark – fork

Vaarm – warm

Vaarmur – warmer

Vaartneit – fortnight

Vaes, vaaees – face

Vaidhur – father

Vaist – feast

Vat – fat

Vaul – fall, veil, fell

Veeld – field

Veeoo – few

Veesh – fish

Veier – fire

Veilit – violet

Vellur – fellow

Ver – far

Vinggur – finger

Vittles – food, provisions or ingredients

Vloi – fly

Voar – afore, before

Vog – fog

Voot – foot

Vorgit – forget

Voul – fowl

Vound – found

Vrog – frog

Vromt – from

Vuirn – fern

Vur – for, or fir

Vurdher – further off

Vurdhist – furthest

Vurray – very

Vurrur – furrow

W

Waaeet – weight

Waak – walk

Waal – well

Waar – war

Waark – work

Wait – wheat

Warm – worm

Wedher – castrated ram

Weeout – without

Wer – was, were

Werret – to worry or a worry

Wet – weight

Widhee – willow

Wik – week

Wikkur – neigh, the noise a horse makes

Wind-list – white streak of faint cloud across a clear blue sky

Winker – child who seeks in 'heidee-hoop'

Winsh – wench, girl

Wint – went

Withywind – climbing plant also known as bindweed

Wit'n – will not

Woak – oak

Woald – old

Woald-faashun – old-fashioned

Woar – worn

Wood'n – wouldn't

Woots – would

Wops – wasp

Wot – who, which, what, that

Woz'n (and wozzint) – wasn't

Wuird – word

Wuirk – work

Wust – worst

Wuts – oats

Y

Yaalur – yellow

Yaandur – yonder

Yaaprun – apron

Yaas – yes

Yaeker – acorn

Yaffle – green woodpecker

Yardstack – stack of grain heaves waiting to be threshed

Yeer – here, and ear

Yoa – ewe

Yoorn – yours

Yungin – young one, youngster

Mr William John Jude Grey, Town Crier from 1885 to 1905, Emsworth, Havant. Town criers worked for the public authority and would carry a hand-bell to attract people's attention, and shout the words '*Oyez, Oyez, Oyez!*' before making their announcements. The word '*Oyez*' means 'hear ye', which is a call for silence and attention. '*Oyez*' derives from the Anglo-Norman word for listen.

Hampshire Arts and Museum Service

Z

Zaaeem – same

Zaik – seek

Zaim – seem

Zault – salt

Zay – sea, say

Zayin – saying
Zbeidur – spider
Zeid – side
Zeit – sight
Zelf – self
Zet – sat, sit
Zich – such
Zid, zeed – saw, seen
Zillur – cellar
Zit – to sit
Zizurz – scissors
Zoa – sow
Zoid – side
Zoidur – cider
Zoo – so
Zooner – rather
Zooud – sold
Zouth – south
Zow – sow
Zummit – something

THE VEN'ZON MARK, OR THE LOST CHILD
A NEW FOREST LEGEND

Th' zummer time
Wur in its prime,
And all wur bright and gay;
The bees wur out,
Buzzen about,
All on that zunshine day.

Th' trees did look,
I' th' bubb'len brook,
As thof' they wur at play;
Th' deer did jump
O'er clump and stump
As stood up in their way.

Poor Mary's boy
Wur all her joy,
A happy child wur he:
Ov all bezide
He wur the pride,
But none zo proud az she.

She put 'un down,
The varn among,
Cloze by her cottage door:
And let 'un play,

The livelong day,
Az she had done avore.

A gipzey camp
Wur on the tramp
On dthick unlucky day:
Th' child they zaw
An' spite o' law,
They carr'd 'un vur away.

Th' boy they zed
Had on his head
A mark o' ven'zon there:
And all agreed
It cou'd be zeed
By a partin' ov his hair.

When Mary miss'd
The child she'd kiss'd
And left upon the ground:
Then she did goo
Th' vorest droo
But the boy cou'd ne'er be vound.

She roam'd about
And loud did shout
Among the brakes and vences,
And night and day,

Wur passed dthick way,
Till Mary lost her zenses.

Well, time pass'd on
And years had gone,
But still she roam'd about:
And now't cou'd hear
Ov th' little dear
Az uzed to laaf and zhout.

And all did think
Her on the brink
Ov death, and now't could zave her;
But still she zed,
Wur One o'er hed,
As never 'ood desave her.

For thof' zhe'd weep
When vast azleep
About her darlin' boy,
Yet when she woke
She rarely spoke,
Zo lost wur all her joy.

But zumtimes she
'Ood goo and zee
Th' ztarm in the vorrest wild:
And then they zay

She uz'd to pray
To God, to zend her child.

Th' znow drove vast
I' th' wintry blast,
And all wur cold and drear;
When late one night
I' th' moon's pale light,
A gipzey did appear.

She cry'd and moan'd
And zighed and groan'd,
And loudly did complain,
Of what she'd done,
But one alone
Cou'd aize her vrom her pain.

For oh! she'd cry,
I vearz to die,
Wi' this upon my mind;
Vor I do know,
And zoon can zhow,
Where you your zon may vind.

Poor Mary heard
The gipzey's word,
And tried to understand;
Her zun she told,

Wur a zodger bold,
Vur in a vorren land.

Th' gipzey died,
And Mary cry'd,
Her wretched end to zee;
Vor her no rest
Wur ever blest,
Zo lost to paice wur she.

The darkzome night
Zaw Mary's vlight,
And now't could aize her mind;
But she 'ood goo
The wordle droo,
Her zodger-boy to find.

Vor oh! the zmart
Ov a mother's heart
Can never be beguiled;
'Tis only know'd,
Or can be show'd,
By them az a' lozt a child.

And years did pass;
Time's vleeting glass
Agen turned o'er and o'er;
And all did vear

We ne'er should hear
Ov Mary any more.

At last, in time,
Vrom vorren clime,
The tidens reached our ears;
Th' war wuz o'er,
And we once more,
Wur zafe vrom all our vears.

For then came whoam,
No more to roam,
Both zodgers and their wives –
Thank God they cry'd
We've safe arriv'd,
Wi' th' blessing ov our lives.
Alas! that ever
Man should zever
The dearest ties in life;
Or mother's zun
Zhould from her run,
Or husbun' vrom his wife.

At last there came
A man o' vame,
An officer zo brave;
In battle vield

Wi' zword and zhield
The banner he did wave.

Zo brave wur he
In each degree,
He conquered all his voes;
That then his vriends
To make amends,
Him for their leader chose.

He once wur left
Of zense bereft
Amung the dead and zlain,
And there he lay
Vor one whole day
Vore he ope'd his eyes again.

And when he did
A woman chid
And whispered – 'Zleep once more'
Th' while he slept
Wi' joy she wept,
For zorrur now wur o'er.

When he awoke
His mother spoke
And zed, 'you are my zun,
Your life I've zav'd

41

And God be praised
Vor ge'en me zuch a one.'

'Vor you my zun
And you alone
I've wandered far and near,
And God did zee
My love for thee
And still my heart did cheer.'

'When thy dear hed
Wur zoftly led,
And I tried to zoothe thy pain;
A spot zo dark
I did remark,
That brought thee back again.'

Heard in Hampshire

As you can probably tell from the poem above and a quick glance at the glossary, there are many gypsy words to be found in Hampshire, most likely because for hundreds of years there has been a constant population of gypsies living and working in the New Forest. So, a policeman is a 'gawermush', a scarecrow a 'gallibagger', eggs are 'cackleberries' and a green woodpecker is a 'yaffle'!

Jobs can be described as 'cushy', from 'kushti', meaning good, and a pound in currency is called a 'bar'. The word 'shrammed' – from the Old English 'scrimman', meaning to shrivel – is often still used for cold and shivery. In the New Forest, the expression 'loo see' is still popular, as is 'cruncheon', meaning an informal evening meal, but these words seem to have vanished completely from the general Hampshire vocabulary.

'Cop the needle' in some parts of Hampshire means to get irritated or angry, while if you're 'puggled' you've been given a good hiding (perhaps coming from the word 'pugilist' – boxer?) Sotonians (the name for people from Southampton) often say 'somewhen' when they mean 'sometime', and on the Isle of Wight caterpillars are called 'mallyshags'.

The most popular topic of conversation in the British Isles must be the weather and so there are a lot of folklore ways to interpret it. One Hampshire way of saying that a storm is approaching is 'It looks dark o'er Will's mother's'. Nobody seems to know who Will is or where his mother lives!

'White rain' is a word used to describe the type of rain that falls in sheets, and 'Woodfidley rain', to people who live in Burley in the New Forest, means it's coming from the south-west – where Woodfidley lies.

Botley, a charming village that has existed for over 1,000 years, has its own lovely variation of 'you can't take it with you when you die', which is 'there are no pockets in a shroud'!

Hampshire hops

THE HOP PICKERS RHYME

Hampshire women here are found,
Born and bred on Hampshire ground,
Hampshire hogs and Hampshire honey,
Both are worth a lot of money,
But of all the Hampshire crops,
Far the best are Hampshire hops (ANON)

Hop pickers in the Alton area, early 20th century.
Hampshire Arts and Museum Service

Growing, picking and drying hops was a major business for those in the Alton area, even before they were put to use in the breweries, throughout the 19th century and up until the 1960s. During hop-picking time large numbers of travellers, gypsies and itinerant workers would arrive in Alton; whole families would come from Portsmouth and Southampton, as well as many from London, to spend a few weeks in the fresh air and earn some money. Hop picking usually started in late August or early September and would last about five weeks. The picture shows a family picking hops into a five or six-bushel basket; the basket would then be taken to the 'tally man' for recording before it was emptied into a surplice for transport to the hop kiln.

Hunt meet at the Old Vine public house at Crocker Hill, Fareham showing hunt members, beagles and bystanders, about 1900.
Hampshire Arts and Museum Service

I wonder if an over-indulgence in the product of hops might have been responsible for murder?! The Old Vine pub, situated on the main Fareham to Wickham Road at Crocker Hill, was once the scene of a murder when, in 1924, the landlord, Arthur Gamblin, who possessed a violent temper when drunk, shot his wife Sarah Jane, his son William, his daughter Sarah and then himself. There have been two Old Vines pubs on this site; the original dated back to the days of George III.

Tales from the not so 'New' Forest

The New Forest is a unique and quite fascinating place. Here are some things you might not know about it:

1. The New Forest is not new: it was created in 1079 as a royal hunting ground by William the Conqueror.

2. And it's not really a forest in the modern sense of being completely tree-covered: there are large areas of open heath, bog and grassland, as well as the ancient woodland.

3. New Forest ponies, the area's most famous residents, appear to be wild but they're all owned by people known as 'commoners', whose properties give them historic rights to graze animals.

4. Donkeys, cattle, pigs and sheep also graze freely in the New Forest alongside the ponies.

Approx 3,000 New Forest ponies roam wild across the open heathland and in the forests.

Hampshire Arts and Museum Service

5. The New Forest has some funny and rude-sounding place names including SANDY BALLS, ANTHONY'S BEE BOTTOM, PIG BUSH, BURNT BALLS, SLAP BOTTOM AND LITTLE STUBBY HAT.

6. You can make some really exotic trips without ever leaving the New Forest: there are places called Canada, Bohemia and Normandy!

7. *Sherlock Holmes* author Sir Arthur Conan Doyle, nursing heroine Florence Nightingale and Alice Hargreaves, the inspiration for Lewis Carroll's *Alice in Wonderland*, are all buried in the New Forest.

8. The New Forest has 26 miles or 42km of coastline.

9. It's home to some rare and important plants and animals, including the wild gladiolus, the Dartford warbler, the southern blue damselfly and the sand lizard.

10. The New Forest is one of Britain's newest and smallest National Parks – it was only designated in 2005.

SOME OTHER NEW FOREST STATISTICS

Area: 218 square miles (564 sq km)

Woodland: 86 square miles (222 sq km)

Heathland and grassland: 61 square miles (157 sq km)

Farmland: 57 square miles (147 sq km)

Public footpaths: 141 miles (226 km)

Highest point: 443ft (135m) near Bramshaw

Tallest tree: 178ft (55m), a giant sequoia on the Rhinefield Drive

New Forest fame

TV presenter ESTHER RANTZEN, naturalist and broadcaster CHRIS PACKHAM, motor racing commentator MURRAY WALKER and film critic MARK KERMODE are among those who have local connections , but what about figures from the past?

The creator of *Sherlock Holmes*, author SIR ARTHUR CONAN DOYLE (1869–1930), has connections with several other parts of the country but he's buried in Minstead churchyard. He bought a house in the village late in his life as a holiday home and set parts of his novel *The White Company* in the New Forest.

ALICE LIDDELL, the inspiration for LEWIS CARROLL's Alice in *Alice's Adventures in Wonderland*, lived in Lyndhurst at a house called Cuffnells. She's buried in Lyndhurst churchyard and the mirror from her house – Alice's 'looking-glass' – can be seen at the New Forest Centre in Lyndhurst.

The artist AUGUSTUS JOHN worked and died in Fordingbridge (1928–1961) and is remembered with an impressive statue. Surprisingly, FLORENCE NIGHTINGALE, renowned for her nursing work in the Crimean War and beyond, is buried in St Margaret's churchyard at East Wellow.

SIR CHRISTOPHER COCKERILL, inventor of the hovercraft, lived in Hythe. T.E. LAWRENCE, better known as Lawrence of Arabia, also spent time during his military service in Hythe as well as at Calshot, where one of the buildings is named after him and bears a small commemorative plaque.

WILLIAM GILPIN, remembered as an artist, writer and reformer, was vicar of St John the Baptist Church at East Boldre from 1777 to 1804. He is buried there and has a memorial. Hymn-writer HENRY LYTE (1793–1847) wrote *'Praise my Soul, the King of Heaven'* and *'Abide with Me'* while he was curate at the Church of St Thomas in Lymington.

One of the best-known Forest figures is the most local: HARRY 'BRUSHER' MILLS (1840–1905), the so-called 'snakecatcher'. He lived in an old charcoal burner's hut and made his living from catching snakes for sale to London Zoo. He is buried in St Nicholas churchyard, Brockenhurst, and has a nearby pub named after him.

Brusher Mills, the infamous New Forest snake charmer, 1905.

Hampshire Arts and Museum Service

'Pompey speak'

Portsmouth, a large naval town situated on the south coast of Hampshire, is unusual in the county in that it appears to have its own, very local, dialect. Affectionately known as Pompey speak or Pompey slang, it's quite different from what you might hear spoken in other parts of Hampshire.

The meaning of the word 'Pompey' – which refers to Portsmouth the town as well as being the nickname for its football club – has a range of explanations, some of which include associations with Pompeii and with Bombay! My favourite, however, and the one that seems most logical, is that ships entering Portsmouth harbour have always made an entry in the ships log of 'Pom. P.' as a reference to Portsmouth Point, and this abbreviation is also used on navigational charts.

The story of the origin of Pompey speak is that in the late 1800s and early 1900s the dockyards attracted an influx of East Londoners and the accent is based on 'Dockyard slang'; however, ship workers were also imported from Bristol, so the accent may be a mixture of both London and Bristol dock workers' language. This Bristol flavour might also explain why Pompey speak has a 'fuller' sound than the London version.

Portsmouth Harbour and the Spinnaker Tower.
The Author

Dockyard phrases such as *'matey'* – a shortened version of *'Ma'ties'*, itself an abbreviation of His or Her Majesties' (i.e. sailors) – can be heard widely throughout Portsmouth. Pea soup is called 'London fog' – an inversion of the usual saying where a thick fog is referred to as a 'pea souper', while spotted dick pudding is 'bugs in the bolster'!

'Weee' is commonly used to expresses surprise, while to *'squinny'* is to complain. Towards the end of the 19th century, schoolchildren were taught a riddle: *'What would you rather do:*

52

run a mile, suck a boil or eat a plate of scabs?' The person questioned usually answered *'Run a mile, of course!'* But the correct answer was 'Eat a plate of scabs' as 'scabs' was the local name for winkles – perhaps from the caps that sealed the shells. Kind of puts you off wanting to eat them, doesn't it?!

'Gunna deyn teyn?' asks if you're going into the town centre, while *'Sarfsee'* is locally understood to mean Southsea. And if you're a dope or an idiot, you'll be referred to as a *'dinlo'*, while sailors are often known as *'skates'*.

Historic dockyard

There has been a dockyard in Portsmouth since King Richard I ordered its construction and granted the town its first charter, in 1194. Eighteen years later, his brother King John instructed that the dockyard be enclosed 'by a good and strong wall'. Henry VII had built the world's first dry dock in the dockyard in 1495. Henry VIII made the dockyard the centre of his fleet construction, and when Charles II created the Royal Navy in 1670, he gave Portsmouth the status of Royal Dockyard. With this came new slips, wharves, storehouses and the first stone docks. The Great Ship Basin and six surrounding dry docks – one now occupied by HMS VICTORY and another by the MARY ROSE – remind us of the great age of sail.

HMS Victory, Nelson's flagship in the Battle of Trafalgar and the
only great wooden ship to be so well preserved.

From 1750 to 1850, the yard was at peak production because
of almost continuous war; in 1800, the Royal Navy had
684 ships and the yard was the world's largest industrial
complex! The end of the Napoleonic Wars saw huge
layoffs but luckily the development of steam propulsion
led to more expansion – within twenty years the workforce
trebled and in 1829, the yard built the world's first steam
screw warship, HMS Fox.

Throughout the 19th century factories multiplied and huge
new docks were constructed. By Parliamentary decree,

another 180 acres were added in 1864. HMS COLOSSUS, Portsmouth's first steel ship, was launched in 1882.

The Royal Dockyard's greatest achievement was the construction of the Dreadnoughts at the beginning of the 20th century. HMS DREADNOUGHT, built in record time, was the first major warship with steam turbines. Then came the super-Dreadnought, the first oil-fired battleship, HMS QUEEN ELIZABETH, launched in 1913.

The yard played a crucial role in Britain's success in both world wars. However, because of defence cuts, the frigate HMS ANDROMEDA, launched in 1967, was the last of the 286 Portsmouth-built ships. The 'Royal Dockyard' title disappeared in 1984, but the Naval Base remains the home port of the Royal Navy. Ships based at Portsmouth include the aircraft carriers HMS INVINCIBLE, ILLUSTRIOUS AND ARK ROYAL, Type 42 destroyers, and Type 23 frigates.

The weird but wonderful Winchester Notions

Winchester is famous for its elite boys' public school – Winchester College – which has existed since the 14th century. The boys who attend are known as 'Wykehamists', after the school's founder, William of Wykeham. Winchester College's 'notions' is a good (and in my opinion bizarre!)

example of a very special type of English that can still be found in Hampshire. It's approximately 600 years old, and is the language that a new boy to the school had, and still has, to learn before Christmas, or else!

Winchester
College Chapel,
Photo attributed to
Andrew Powers 18/06/2005

At the beginning of their first term, the Notions Book is sent to 'New Men'. Both 'notions' (to mean words and phrases) and 'men' (to mean boys) are examples of this strange language. Some notions are created by shortening phrases – for example, the Dons' Common Room Notice Board became the 'Do Co Ro No Bo'; other notions come from Latin – for example, foricas (Latin for 'lavatory') was shortened to 'fo'. So a pupil might comment, 'It's fortunate that the Do Co Ro has its own Fo'!

Below is a sample of Winchester College's Notions. A few of these can now be found in other UK public schools, such as Eton and Harrow, but most are unique to Winchester.

Abroad – out of the sick room

Backings-up – old pieces of faggot ends put onto a low fire in college

Bake – to sit or lie at ease

Battlings – money supplied weekly to the boys

Bibbling – a flogging of six strokes

Blow – to blush

Bogle (sometimes bogwheel) – bicycle

Bread-pickers – juniors appointed by the four senior prefects to put candles in outhouses

Brock – to bully or tease

Cargo – hamper of eatables sent to a boy from his friends

Chinner – a grin

Chisel – to cheat

Clow – box on the ear

Continent – confined to the sick room – opposite of 'abroad'

Cud – pretty

Div – class or form

Duck – the face

Ferk – expel, send away

Firk – old dialect word meaning to expel, which gave rise to a legend that an expelled pupil had his clothes handed to him through the gate by the Old Mill on a pitchfork (Latin furca)

Flyer – half-volley kick at football

Fo – toilet

Glope – to spit

Jig – a clever man

Jubilee – a pleasant time

Junket – exclamation of self-congratulation

Kill – to hurt badly

Knuckle down – kneel down

Lobster – to cry

Logie – sewage

Man – pupil (of any age); always used instead of boy

Mug – to work, giving the name Mugging Hall to the room in every house (except college) where work is done in Toys. 'Mugging down' is working in the evenings

Mug – to study

Mugster – one who mugs

Muttoner – a blow to the knuckles from a cricket ball

Non licet – forbidden (thus 'Non Licet Gate' which used to be for pupils who were expelled, as they were not permitted through Outer Gate)

Notions – the words in the word-book

Ponto – a piece of bread kneaded into a ball

Poser – an examiner

Quill – to curry favour

Rabbiter – a blow on the back of the neck with the side of the hand

Rem – remedy (usually shortened to 'rem', most notably in 'half-rem'), meaning a day's holiday, derived from Latin remedium, rest or refreshment

Scadger – a rascal

Schitt – a goal at football!

Scob – a type of chest used as a desk, thought to come from Latin scabellum, but 19th-century notions books explain it as the sound of 'box' backwards!

Scrubbing – a flogging of four strokes

Shuffle – to act a part, deceive

Smuggler – small lead pencil pointed at both ends

Socius – a companion

Solo – a walk without a socius!

Splice – to throw a missile

Squish – weak tea

Straw – clean sheets

Stuckling – a pudding made of meat, apple and caraway (yuk!)

Sus – remains of a Prefect's tea passed on to their valets in college

Sweater – a servant

Toll – run

Toys – a small bookcase and desk combined

Toytime – homework or prep

Word-book – dictionary of Notions
Worms – line cut in the turf as a goal-line at football

Old 'Wykehamists' include writer ANTHONY TROLLOPE (The Barchester Chronicles), the British fascist leader SIR OSWALD MOSLEY, famous cricketer DOUGLAS JARDINE, film director and screenwriter JOSS WHEEDON (creator of *Buffy the Vampire Slayer* and writer of *Toy Story* and *Alien Resurrection*) and JON WRIGHT, founder of Innocent Smoothies – perhaps he invented smoothies as a protest against the 'squish' he would have been served at Winchester College!

And, in sharp contrast to the Wykehamists, here's a shouting rhyme that apparently every Hampshire schoolchild used to know (and not a single Latin reference to be found in it!)

Where be yon blackbird to?
I know where he be.
He be up yon wurzel tree
And I be a'ter ee.
He sees I,
I sees ee,
Ee knows I be a'ter ee.
With a bloody gert stick I'll knock ee down.
Blackbird! I'll ave ee!

Pupils dancing in the playground, St Joseph's Catholic School, Havant 1920s.
Hampshire Arts and Museum Service

'Us and Them'?

This poem tells us that the author (unfortunately anonymous) was cynically aware of the class differences existing in Hampshire!

O, come and live in Chandler's Ford
Among the pampas grasses
And climb the pinnacle of pretence
Among the middle classes

What joy, what joy we all do feel
When first we cross the border
And leave dark Eastleigh's meanest streets
To all the lower order

We triple glaze each window
And insulate our loft
Lest cold winds blow and evil draughts
Prevent our getting soft

Suburban man does swell with pride
And fills his heart with glee
When unlike Eastleigh's stone-flagged yards
His garden grows a tree

So have your wretched little lives
And all your seven-year itches
Do come and live in Chandler's Ford
And be bigger than your breeches ANON

Incidentally, Chandler's Ford made national headlines when an armed bank robbery was foiled. On 13 September 2007, the Metropolitan Police's Flying Squad, along with the Hampshire Constabulary, foiled a bank robbery outside the HSBC Bank in the central shopping precinct. Two robbers were shot dead by the police after they were tipped off about the robbery and hid behind the nearby toilet cubicles. One more robber fled the scene by car but was later arrested.

What's in a name?

There are about 300 place names in Hampshire, and their origins contain a wealth of history and romance. All 300 are worth exploring, but that would take another book! So let's just look at a few examples.

In the west of the county is **Broughton**. According to The Complete Atlas of the British Isles, England has thirteen villages called Broughton. The name means either 'Brook Farm' or 'The Farm by the Fort'. In the case of our Broughton, 'Brook Farm' is most relevant. The first part of the name, 'Brough', comes from the Saxon word broc, which then meant fast-flowing stream, and has become our modern word 'brook'. The second part of the name comes from the Saxon word tun, which progressively meant a farm, a hamlet, a village and finally a town.

In the middle of Hampshire is the village of **Micheldever** on the River Dever. In the ninth century the name was recorded as Mycendefr. Linguists think this is a Celtic name and the meaning appears to be 'boggy waters'. The second part of the name, defr, means 'stream'. So River Dever means River River! That's not unusual, though; the Avon and Ouse are also old Britonnic words meaning 'river' so the River Avon is also the River River, as is the River Ouse.

To the east of the county, and towards the end of the alphabet, is the village of **Sheet**. It's on the River Rother and the name comes from the Old English word sciete, meaning a 'projecting piece of land, corner, or nook'. It was so named because it's located on the angle between two streams. The larger stream is called the Rother, an interesting name in itself. It's the name of a bridge that once went over it – 'rother' comes from Old English hryther, meaning cattle. So it was once simply the cattle bridge.

To the north of the county is **Basingstoke**. This name is made up of three Old English elements: *Basa* + *inga* + *stoc*. Basa is the name of a Saxon leader. Inga is an element that appears in many English place names, and usually means possession of a place by the people led by the named person. Stoc means 'outlying farmstead'. Putting all these together, Basingstoke means the place where you'll find the isolated farm owned by the people once led by Basa! John Arlott, the famous voice of cricket with a much-loved 'Hampshire burr', called his autobiography Basingstoke Boy, because he was brought up in the then pretty market town in the early 20th century. The fact that he was born so far to the north of the county shows the range and strength of the accent before the arrival of Basingstoke's 'London overspill' population in the 1960s.

And what about **Winchester**, the city at the centre of the county and its history? The Romans named the settlement they found there Venta Belgarum, meaning 'Chief Place of the Belgae'. Belgae was what the Romans called Britons living in the area now called Hampshire, having previously met these people in what is now called Belgium. The Romans set up military fortifications at the Chief Place of the Belgae, and the Roman word for those fortifications was castra – camps. When the Romans left in AD 410, the newly arrived Saxons called the city Wintanceastre, pronouncing castra as 'chester'. There are many 'chesters' in England – Manchester, Colchester, Dorchester, Chichester, Winchester, Portchester, Rochester. They were all once Roman fortifications. The Saxons didn't have a 'v' sound, and they pronounced the Roman 'v' as 'w', so 'Venta Castra' became 'Winta-chester', and over many years it has morphed into present-day Winchester.

Buckler's Hard, famous for shipbuilding; some of the ships of Admiral Nelson's fleet were constructed here.
The Author

Buckler's Hard: a 'hard' is an area of shoreline that is sufficiently firm, either naturally or by human effort, to give easy access to boats moored along it. In the days when heavy items, such as cargo and cannon, needed to be moved between the ship and shore, solid ground was an important consideration, and there was not always a wharf available. Buckler's Hard was developed as a double row of workers' cottages with a broad working area, or 'hard', between them that led down to the river. From the 17th century onwards all prime timber in Hampshire was reserved for the Navy and much of it went to Portsmouth and other naval dockyards. However, many British naval vessels, including several of Admiral Nelson's fleet, for instance HMS AGAMEMNON, were built at Buckler's Hard. The AGAMEMNON was a Royal

Navy third-rate 'ship of the line' with an armament of 64 guns. She was launched in 1781, and served until 1809 when she was lost after running aground on a shoal in the mouth of the River Plate. Although ship building declined at Buckler's Hard in the 19th century, the tradition is not completely lost, and a company building motor yachts now occupies the Agamemnon Yard.

Alton, meaning simply 'old town', was mentioned earlier in relation to hop picking and its renowned breweries, but also has a church famous for being the scene of a heroic battle in 1643 when the Royalist Captain JOHN BOLLE took refuge with his men and refused to surrender. He was killed as he fought in the pulpit and the damage caused by the gunshot can still be seen in the church door today.

Church of St Lawrence, Alton, circa 1830.
Creative Commons

ALTONIA

Upon a Hampshire Hill I stand
Surrounded by the verdant land
Beneath in yonder vale I see
A little town well known to me

See yonder ancient building grey
There the people come to pray
And there the Royalists refuge found
When rebel hosts were all around

And while I'm standing gazing here
I think of many visions dear
There on my right a wood called Great
Where boys and girls hold many a fete

And a green hill down below
Near which a silvery stream doth flow
And at the back of that Lynch hill
Where children pluck wild flowers at will

See by the Butts that leafy road
To Selborne, Gilbert White's abode
And many a lovely walk is found
Near sweet Altona town so fair.

S.R. BICKERTON, JULY 1892

The Reverend Gilbert White referred to in this poem was a famous naturalist. He believed in studying living birds and animals in their natural habitat, which was an unusual approach at that time, as most naturalists preferred to carry out detailed examinations of dead specimens in the comfort of their studies. White was the first to distinguish the chiffchaff, willow warbler and wood warbler as three separate species, largely due to their different songs, and he was the first to accurately describe the harvest mouse and the noctule bat. There's a very interesting museum dedicated to his work in the town of Selborne where he lived.

Less pleasantly, Alton is associated with the saying 'Sweet Fanny Adams'. This was the name of an eight-year-old girl who was murdered in a nearby hop field in 1867. The trial of the murderer and the extensive press coverage of the horrible details coincided with the introduction of a much-disliked tinned mutton in the Royal Navy. The sailors compared the contents of the tins to the remains of the murdered girl and eventually, 'Sweet Fanny Adams' (or 'Sweet FA') came to mean 'nothing of substance at all'!

HMS Havant, the Royal Navy ship sunk in June 1940 while
evacuating troops from the beaches at Dunkirk.
Hampshire Arts and Museum Service

Farnborough, where I live now, means merely 'hill overgrown
with ferns' – nothing could be further from the truth! World-
famous for its air show, which brings tens of thousands of
visitors to the town, it was once a village but grew with the
military and now merges with the neighbouring Army town
of Aldershot. What is less known about it, though, is that it's
the unlikely place where the Napoleonic dynasty came to an
end! Napoleon III and Princess Eugenie fled to England in
1870 after the disastrous Franco-Prussian war. Three years
later the Emperor died and his widow moved to Farnborough
and acquired Farnborough Hill. In 1887 she built a huge
mausoleum. In a vaulted crypt there are three impressive
granite sarcophagi, one each for the Emperor, their son the
Prince Imperial, who died fighting British troops in the Zulu

war, and one for herself. She died in 1920 aged 94. She also established St Michael's Abbey at the same location, which today is still run by Benedictine monks.

Princess Eugenie's tomb, St Michael's Abbey, Farnborough.
Creative Commons

Hampshire's small claims to fame

Bats: The attractive village of Greywell stands at the mouth of the one-mile (1.6km) long tunnel on the Basingstoke Canal. About quarter of a mile (400m) in, the tunnel has collapsed and is now home to the largest bat roost in Europe!

Rabbits: A spectacular viewpoint on the Hampshire hills near Kingsclere is Watership Down. This is where Hazel the rabbit and his friends come to live after their adventures in Richard Adams' novel of the same name. Adams was born near here and set his best-selling book in the beautiful countryside he remembered exploring as a boy.

Tombs and TV: In the remains of an old iron-age fort on Beacon Hill, a high point of the north Hampshire Downs, is the grave of the 5th Earl of Carnarvon. He paid for the expedition that discovered the tomb of Tutankhamun in the Valley of the Kings in 1922. He died in Cairo shortly afterwards, some say as a result a curse: *'Death will slay with his wings whoever disturbs the peace of the Pharaoh.'* Beacon Hill overlooks the Earl's home, Highclere Castle, which is famous today as the location of TV's DOWNTON ABBEY!

Noteworthy Hampshire folk: Famous Victorian author CHARLES DICKENS (*David Copperfield, Nicholas Nickleby, The Pickwick Papers*, and *A Christmas Carol*, among many others) was born in Portsmouth; he was forced to leave school at a relatively early age to work in a factory when his father was thrown into debtors' prison. JANE AUSTEN (*Pride and Prejudice, Mansfield Park, Emma, Sense and Sensibility*) was born in Steventon in the north-east of the county and spent much of her life in Hampshire; she is buried in Winchester Cathedral.

Jane Austen
Creative Commons

Pre-Raphaelite painter SIR JOHN EVERETT MILLAIS was born in Southampton and has a gallery in the town named after him. Other well-known people born in Southampton include comedian BENNY HILL, film director KEN RUSSELL, singer/songwriter HOWARD JONES, and TV gardener CHARLIE DIMMOCK.

Other famous Portsmouth people include: *Sherlock Holmes* author and one-time Portsmouth FC goalkeeper, SIR ARTHUR CONAN DOYLE; engineer ISAMBARD KINGDOM BRUNEL (the famous builder of bridges), and former Prime Minister JAMES CALLAGHAN.

Thirsty work!

It's often possible to discover a little more about a location by looking at the history of some of the local pubs. Hampshire is no exception, and here are just a few with a tale to tell.

The White Horse Inn at Priors Dean is known locally as 'The Pub With No Name', because it has no sign and because of its remoteness, which made it very difficult to find for much of the last century. The pub was the local of World War I poet Edward Thomas, and was immortalised in his poem *'Up in the Wind'*; here are a couple of verses:

'I could wring the old thing's neck that put it here!
A public-house! it may be public for birds,
Squirrels, and suchlike, ghosts of charcoal-burners
And highwaymen.' The wild girl laughed. 'But I
Hate it since I came back from Kennington.
I gave up a good place.' Her Cockney accent
Made her and the house seem wilder by calling up –
Only to be subdued at once by wildness –
The idea of London, there in that forest parlour,
Low and small among the towering beeches,
And the one bulging butt that's like a font.

Her eyes flashed up; she shook her hair away
From eyes and mouth, as if to shriek again;
Then sighed back to her scrubbing. While I drank
I might have mused of coaches and highwaymen,
Charcoal-burners and life that loves the wild.
For who now used these roads except myself,
A market wagon every other Wednesday,
A solitary tramp, some very fresh one
Ignorant of these eleven houseless miles,
A motorist from a distance slowing down
To taste whatever luxury he can
In having North Downs clear behind, South clear before,
And being midway between two railway lines,
Far out of sight or sound of them? There are
Some houses – down the by-lanes; and a few
Are visible – when their damsons are in bloom.
But the land is wild, and there's a spirit of wildness
Much older, crying when the stone-curlew yodels
His sea and mountain cry, high up in Spring.
He nests in fields where still the gorse is free as
When all was open and common. Common 'tis named
And calls itself, because the bracken and gorse
Still hold the hedge where plough and scythe have chased them.
Once on a time 'tis plain that the 'White Horse'
Stood merely on the border of waste
Where horse and cart picked its own course afresh.

On all sides then, as now, paths ran to the inn;
And now a farm-track takes you from a gate.

EDWARD THOMAS, 1914, extract, from The First World War
Poetry Digital Archive, University of Oxford.
www.oucs.ox.ac.uk/ww1lit

The Pub with No Name

The Still and West Country House – this pub is situated
at the very edge of the harbour entrance in Old Portsmouth;
you can watch warships and cross-channel ferries pass
within inches of you as you sup your pint!

The Jolly Sailor, on the River Humble at Burleson, is the pub featured in the 1980s BBC TV soap Howards' Way.

The Bat and Ball at Hambledon is the birthplace of English cricket. The village team was exceptionally talented and became famous for inflicting an innings defeat on an all-England side in 1777. The founder of Lord's Cricket Ground, SIR THOMAS LORD, is buried at nearby West Meon. His much-loved 'Hampshire burr' was typical of the local accent.

The Bat and Ball, Hambledon – birthplace of English cricket.
The Author

Well, that's it from me – the pubs are open! I hope that you've enjoyed reading, as much as I've enjoyed compiling, this very brief exploration of Hampshire, its dialects, places and some of its history, old and new.

Bibliography

Collected Memories of Hampshire: Personal Memories inspired by the Francis Frith Collection, 2013, The Francis Frith Collection.

The Complete Atlas of the British Isles, The Reader's Digest Association, London, Sydney, Montreal, Cape Town, 1965.

Hampshire and the Isle of Wight, DAVID HINTON and DR A.N. NOBLE, 1988, George Philip/Ordnance Survey.

I Never Knew That about England, CHRISTOPHER WINN, 2005, Random House Group.

Tales of the New Forest, PHILLIP KLITZ, 1850, accessible at www.klitzandsons.co.uk/philip.htm

The Dialect of the New Forest in Hampshire, SIR JAMES WILSON, KCSI, 1913, Oxford University Press

Victorian and Edwardian Hampshire, BARRY STAPLETON, 2008, Amberley Publishing

www.englishproject.org/resources/english-language-hampshire (accessed 6 May 2014)

http://en.wikipedia.org/w/index.php?title=English_in_southern_England#Hampshire (accessed 3 May 2014)

www3.hants.gov.uk/austen/deane-parsonage.htm
(accessed 3 May 2014)

www.winchestercollege.org/notions-winchester-glossary
(accessed 30 April 2014)

www.newforestpics.co.uk/section499696_178387.html
(accessed 6 May 2014)

www.mygosport.org/info_pages_htm/gosport_history.htm
(accessed 6 May 2014)